A Guide Back to *You*

A workbook for exploring who you are

and staying true to yourself

Maureen Kane, MA, LMHC, LCPC

A Guide Back to *You*

A workbook for exploring who you are

and staying true to yourself

Maureen Kane, MA, LMHC, LCPC

Gray Matter Press
Seattle Los Angeles

Gray Matter Press

The Brain Initiative, Inc.

www.the-brain-initiative.com

ISBN: 8-9862415-1-7
ISBN-13: 979-8-9862415-1-7

A Guide Back to You: A Workbook for Exploring Who You Are and Staying True to Yourself

Maureen Kane 1st ed.

Book design and cover design by Seán Dwyer

This workbook is dedicated to all the clients I have had the privilege to work with as they explored these and other questions. Their courage pushed me to find responses to their needs and expand my tool kit. Also, thank you to my husband, Sean, who championed this book and has volunteered for the unique experience of marrying a therapist.

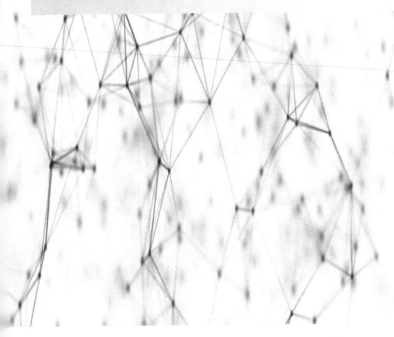

The time will come
when, with elation
you will greet yourself arriving
at your own door, in your own mirror
and smile at each other's welcome...
--From the poem "Love After Love" by Derek Walcott

CONTENTS

A Guide Back to *You*

A workbook for exploring who you are and staying true to yourself

We all struggle at times to know who we are and what we want. Life transitions and our upbringing can make the issue more challenging. I hear about this issue in my psychotherapy practice often. You might relate to some of the thoughts clients have shared with me.

- Jane told me, "I've spent my whole marriage trying to be who I thought he wanted, and now I don't even know who I am any more."

- Toby said, "Now that I've retired and I'm not 'a manager,' I don't know what I want to do, or even what I like to do. I've lost my purpose."

- Julie cried while she shared, "Growing up, my mom would tell me I wasn't feeling what I was. Now I don't trust my thoughts or feelings."

- Mark and Kelly came to therapy because they are new empty-nesters and are struggling with their identity as individuals and as a couple now that they aren't parenting daily.

- Jamie came to therapy because they are graduating from college and feel lost about their next steps.

- Megan worried, "As I age and my body changes, I don't recognize myself. I wonder if I even have any worth any more."

I looked around for a workbook to share with these clients and couldn't find anything, so I decided to write it.

In this workbook you will find exercises that my clients have successfully used to explore who they are, what they want, and how to stay true to themselves.

How to Use This Workbook

Just as you will be finding your unique self, your way of working will be unique. I suggest starting with the centering chapter before doing any of the exercises and using those practices before you try each activity.

Beyond that, feel free to go in order or jump to exercises that appeal to you. Different ones may attract you or fit you better at different times. Each provides a mirror reflecting who you are. The more you do, the more you will discover. However, there is no need to complete them all or do them in any order.

My wish for you is that you will have a fun and creative journey towards trusting yourself and your unique path.

START WITH CENTERING

It's tough to know who we are and what we want if we are scattered. The following exercises can help you feel grounded and centered. They can be very helpful throughout the day, so you don't lose track of yourself or your wants and needs.

I suggest that you perform one of the centering practices before you do any exercises in this book, so you are coming from a calm and clear place.

Try a few and see which seems to work best for you. Or mix them up if you get bored.

Container

Let's create an imaginary container to hold the things that distract you, just for the time you want to work in this workbook. This is also a great exercise for other times when something may be on your mind, but you need to focus at the moment.

Create a container in your mind – it can be anything: a canning jar, a shipping container, a basket. Fill the inside with things that will keep your distractions comfortable so they can stay there for a while. You might put in a beanbag chair and video games or favorite animals or people. Whatever you think would keep your worries and distractions comfortable so they will stay there.

Next, decide where your container will live. On a shelf in your home? On the moon? Wherever feels right.

Now sit quietly and allow all your worries and distractions to gently go into the container. Promise them you will work with them another time. (Sometimes the things simply take care of themselves while in your container.) Close the container and send it off to where it lives.

Take a moment to notice how you feel in your mind and body after this exercise and write a few notes about your container and your experience.

CARD BOARD BOX ON THE MOON

More thoughts?

Diaphragmatic Breathing

When we breathe in a shallow way, it contributes to anxiety and feeling scattered or unclear. Diaphragmatic breathing calms our nervous system (by stimulating the vagus nerve) and gives us better access to the creative parts of our brains.

Begin by sitting tall or lying down.
Place your hands on your lower belly.
Gently breathe all the way down into your lower belly. You should feel your hands rise a little bit.
Exhale and feel your hands fall towards your spine.
(Breathe gently or you may get dizzy).

Once you have the hang of this type of breath, use this sequence:

1. Breathe in for a count of four.
2. Hold for a count of two.
3. Exhale for a count of six.

You can experiment with the counts; just make sure your exhale is longer than your inhale. A long exhale tells our nervous system that we are safe, and we can relax.

Take a moment to notice how you feel in your mind and body after doing this. Feel free to write a few notes.

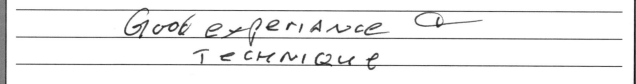

Good experiance a
Technique

More thoughts!

It's very difficult to know ourselves if we are ruminating on the past or worried about the future. This exercise helps ground us in the here and now so we can show up as ourselves. (It's also a great tool for managing panic attacks and anxiety.) We will use our senses to ground in the here and now.

Follow along:

Slowly notice and name (out loud if you can) five things you see.
1.
2.
3.
4.
5.

Slowly notice and name (out loud if you can) five things you hear. You can repeat things if you don't hear five.
1.
2.
3.
4.
5.

Slowly notice and name (out loud if you can) five things you feel. This is not feelings like happy or mad, but tactile feelings like. "I feel my hair brushing my neck. I feel the texture of the table I am touching. I feel my back against my chair."
1.
2.
3.
4.
5.

Now we drop to four.

Slowly notice and name (out loud if you can) four things you see.
1.
2.
3.
4.

Slowly notice and name (out loud if you can) four things you hear. You can repeat things if you don't hear four.

1.
2.
3.
4.

Slowly notice and name (out loud if you can) four things you feel. This is not feelings like happy or mad, but tactile feelings like. "I feel my hair brushing my neck. I feel the texture of the table I am touching. I feel my back against my chair."

1.
2.
3.
4.

Now we drop to three.

Slowly notice and name (out loud if you can) three things you see.

1.
2.
3.

Slowly notice and name (out loud if you can) three things you hear.

1.
2.
3.

Slowly notice and name (out loud if you can) three things you feel.

1.
2.
3.

Now we drop to two.

Slowly notice and name (out loud if you can) two things you see.
1.
2.

Slowly notice and name (out loud if you can) two things you hear.
1.
2.

Slowly notice and name (out loud if you can) two things you feel.
1.
2.

And now one of each.

A thing I see.
1.

A thing I hear.
1.

A thing I feel.
1.

Take a moment to notice how you feel in your mind and body. Do you feel more present? Are you less focused on the past or future? Feel free to jot down a few notes.

TAUGHT TO me by SALly

Love IT when PANICING

More thoughts?

Mindful Walking:

Some people struggle with sitting still or simply prefer to move. No problem. Just get up and have a short, mindful walk in your home or outside. Notice one thing at a time. Here are some options.

1. Notice your footfalls, how your foot moves from heel to toe.
2. Notice colors. How many blue things do you see, red things? How many shades? What are the shadows doing?
3. Notice sounds. How many sounds can you hear? Are they near or far? Can you notice the quiet between sounds?
4. Notice sensations. How does the air feel on your skin, what smells are there, what is the texture under your feet, how does that leaf feel?

Take a moment to notice how you feel in your mind and body after this activity. Feel free to jot down a few notes.

_____

_____

_____

_____

_____

_____

_____

_____

_____

_____

_____

_____

_____

_____

_____

_____

_____

More thoughts!

What Did You Love to Do as a Child?

Children have a better sense of what they like than most adults. What did you love to do? What does that say about who you are?

- Sheila would spend hours organizing papers and drawers and toys. She now enjoys working at a bank and keeping track of loans and spreadsheets.

- Henry loved to take things apart, much to the chagrin of his family! Henry became an engineer because he loves to know how things work.

- Nancy would sneak out of school to play in the woods. She had trouble sitting still. Nancy found a great vocational fit as a park maintenance worker.

What did you love to do? What qualities in you came alive when you did those things?

I loved to_____ as a child	Qualities in me that came alive
Go camping	*Figuring out how to cook and put up a tent (solving puzzles), singing*
Make crafts	*Creativity, solving puzzles*
Reading	*Imagination, comfort in being alone and thinking*

It's your turn:

I loved to_____ as a child	Qualities in me that came alive

I loved to_____ as a child	Qualities in me that came alive

Our "Giveaway"

Dr Rachel Naomi Remen has spoken of a wonderful idea: that each of us has a Giveaway based on our uniqueness. In nature, everything has and knows its Giveaway. Trees provide oxygen, food, and shelter for animals. Water is a home to animals and nourishes and grows plants. We humans struggle with our Giveaway.

Our Giveaway is not the same as our vocation. In fact, we can bring our Giveaway to any job. For example, being a writer is not a Giveaway, but people who write might have any of the following Giveaways:

- I help people think about deep ideas
- I give information to people
- I stir up the status quo
- I connect strangers to each other
- I point out injustice
- I comfort the dying
- I celebrate beauty
- I help people feel important

There are likely hundreds more possible Giveaways that a writer might have. So let go of the idea of vocation and just explore your essence.

Dr. Remen says we all have one main Giveaway. I believe mine is to see the best in people and help them discover and use their gifts. Let's explore what yours might be.

Here are some markers of what you might feel when in your Giveaway.

Giveaway Markers:
- ☐ An experience of Joy or Meaning
- ☐ Feels courageous
- ☐ Feels effortless
- ☐ Sense of being the right person in the right place (even without others' approval)
- ☐ Feeling in flow
- ☐ Grateful you are doing it
- ☐ Brings you joy even if it's not received
- ☐ Feeling of belonging
- ☐ Feels natural

Write about a time when you felt these things:

- What were you doing?
- Who were you doing them with?
- How did you feel?
- What effect did it have on you?
- What barriers did you have to confront?

_____

_____

_____

_____

_____

_____

_____

_____

_____

_____

_____

_____

_____

_____

_____

_____

_____

_____

_____

_____

_____

_____

_____

_____

What might the moment you wrote about tell you about your Giveaway?

Linda felt Giveaway Markers when she led meetings at work. When she explored why, it wasn't about the meeting or the people in it. In fact, the people in the meeting were very challenging for her. In this meeting, however, Linda found that she could weave together a lot of ideas and create something new that had never been considered before. Linda thinks that her Giveaway is "idea weaver."

_____
_____
_____
_____
_____
_____
_____
_____
_____
_____
_____
_____
_____
_____
_____
_____
_____
_____
_____
_____
_____
_____
_____
_____
_____
_____
_____

Bring this exercise to someone who knows you and ask what they think. Make notes about their impressions of what the time you wrote about might say about you.

_____

_____

_____

_____

_____

_____

_____

_____

_____

_____

_____

_____

_____

_____

_____

_____

_____

_____

_____

_____

_____

_____

_____

_____

_____

_____

_____

_____

Find an Object

Sometimes objects can speak to us in subconscious ways. Carl Jung says symbols are a complete language in themselves. They help us see the unseen. They help us bring the unconscious to focus.

Look around your home or go outside and choose an object that speaks to you. Don't work too hard at it or second guess it.

Sit with that object and wonder into what it says to you about your Giveaway.

John chose a knife and found that he loves to cut to the truth of things. He is the one who is unafraid to say what he sees, and you know he is honest when he speaks.

Sadie chose a rose pinecone. These are the kind that look like a flower, and the 'petals' fall away to reveal the seed. Sadie is interested in the heart of things. She sees deeply into people's gifts and brings them to life.

What is your object saying to you?

_____
_____
_____
_____
_____
_____
_____
_____
_____
_____
_____
_____
_____
_____
_____
_____

Look again at the items you surround yourself with at work, home, and school. Purposefully use them as reminders of how you want to show up.

_____
_____
_____
_____
_____
_____
_____
_____
_____
_____
_____
_____
_____
_____
_____
_____
_____
_____
_____
_____
_____
_____
_____
_____
_____
_____
_____
_____
_____

Family Stories

Family stories are a wonderful clue to our Giveaway, but not on face value. Is there a story your family tells about you? Let's mine it for gifts.

Rachel says when she was young, her mother brought home a dead fish for dinner. Rachel was so taken by the plight of this fish that she held it for two days. The family tells this as a funny story, but Rachel came to see it as her Giveaway of protecting and loving life. She eventually became a doctor.

Margaret was called a "magpie" growing up. They would take things from their siblings' bedrooms and arrange them in their own. Margaret grew up to become a spiritual director and draws from all traditions in their work.

What are your family stories, and what might they say about you in a new way?

_____

_____

_____

_____

_____

_____

_____

_____

_____

_____

_____

_____

_____

_____

_____

_____

_____

_____

_____

More thoughts?

Journey to a Wise Person

Try this guided meditation and see what information may come to you.

Sit or lie down with your eyes closed. You may like some peaceful music (without words) to keep you company. Start with the diaphragmatic breathing on page 12.

Imagine walking along a forest path or some other lovely place where you feel peace. Ask for a friend of your Giveaway to show up. (This could be someone who can tell you more about your Giveaway or a part of yourself that may have something to tell you.) Trust who or whatever comes; they may be real or fictional, living or not.

Ask them:

- What do you think my Giveaway is?
- What beliefs about myself might get in the way of my knowing or acting on it?
- What would you like me to know about my Giveaway that I don't know now?
- Ask for a gift to remind you of your Giveaway.

When you are finished, gently open your eyes and write down what you experienced.

_____
_____
_____
_____
_____
_____
_____
_____
_____
_____
_____
_____
_____
_____
_____
_____

More thoughts!

Our Bodies Know the Truth

Checking in with our bodies can be a great way to know our truth when we are unsure. Give this a try.

- Start with the diaphragmatic breathing on page 12.
- Now, settle into your body.
- Notice your seat in the chair (if you are sitting).
- Notice your feet on the ground.
- Notice what it feels like *inside* your hands. You might feel pulsing, vibrations, heat, coolness, or something else.
- What does it feel like inside your feet?
- Inside your chest?
- Inside your stomach?
- Inside your pelvis?

When you feel like you've arrived in your body, say out loud or to yourself something that you know to be true for you.

It could be "*My name is _____*" or "*I love my cat.*" Whatever feels true.

Carefully notice what you sense in your body when you state a truth for you. Some people may feel larger, more solid, a warm or bubbly feeling, or their posture shifts. It is unique to each person.

Now repeat the exercise with something you know to be untrue for you. The more untrue the better.

Carefully notice what you feel in your body when you state an untruth for you. Some people may feel their throat tighten, feel cold, feel smaller, feel an upset in their stomach, or feel their face scrunch. It will be unique to you.

Try it a few times and make some notes. Now you have an internal truth detector.

Truth: I love being outdoors	Untruth: I want to punch a kitten today
What I notice in my body:	What I notice in my body:
I feel sort of expansive	*I feel prickly*
I notice my heart area feels warm.	*I feel very slightly nauseated*
I am smiling	*My face is scrunched up*

It's your turn:

Truth	Untruth
What I notice in my body:	What I notice in my body:

Truth	Untruth
What I notice in my body:	What I notice in my body:

Truth	Untruth
What I notice in my body:	What I notice in my body:

Truth	Untruth
What I notice in my body:	What I notice in my body:

Truth	Untruth
What I notice in my body:	What I notice in my body:

What Would You Do if You Weren't Afraid?

Sometimes we hold back from expressing who we are because of our fears.

Set a timer for 10 minutes and write about this. Just keep answering the question: **What would I do if I weren't afraid?**

Don't stop. If you don't know what to write, write *I don't know what to write.*

After you are finished, see what you might be hiding under fear. Do you want to do anything differently now that you know what you would do if you weren't afraid?

What I would do if I weren't afraid

_____

_____

_____

_____

_____

_____

_____

_____

_____

_____

_____

_____

_____

_____

_____

_____

_____

_____

_____

_____ →

Keep Thinking!

Almost there!

Examining Your Values

Our values are an important compass for how we navigate the world and an expression of who we are. When we are clear on our values, our decisions become easier because we can ask, "Does this decision align with my values?"

Let's get some clarity about your values.

The following is a list of many values, along with blank spaces to write in your own. Go ahead and cut them into cards or copy them onto your own cards. Think carefully about each one and sort it under the value categories (page 63).

First sort for: Are they your value? Not your value? Discard the ones that are not your values. Using the remaining cards, sort them by how important they are to you. Is it a value you believe you *should* have? If so, do you want to make it one, or do you want to let go of the *should?*

Then look at your values by setting (page 64). Are they the same when you are at work or school? In your family and relationships? In your leisure time? In your self-care time? In your spiritual life (if that is important to you)?

Lastly, rank them on the pyramid (pages 65-67) by most important at the top to lesser but important values in the lower rungs.

Once you have some clarity, you can use them to help guide your decisions and sense of self.

For example, *Claire found herself saying yes to every social invitation, but often found herself overwhelmed, tired, and spending a lot of money.*

When she did her values ranking, Claire found that she values *connection, empathy,* and *responsibility.* Using these values as her compass, she began to evaluate social invitations. She experimented with saying yes to invitations that brought her connection, and no to those that did not and/or would cost her money beyond her budget. Following these guidelines, Claire found that her social life became richer and enjoyable again.

Look for the cards beginning on page 39.

Accepting	Accomplishment
Admiration	Adventure
Affection	Ambition
Appreciation	Approval
Attentive	Authority
Autonomy	Balance
Beauty	Belonging

Accomplishment	Accepting
Adventure	Admiration
Ambition	Affection
Approval	Appreciation
Authority	Attentive
Balance	Autonomy
Belonging	Beauty

Calm	Capable
Caring	Challenge
Change	Cleanliness
Comfort	Commitment
Compassion	Competition
Connection	Cooperation
Courage	Creativity

Capable	Calm
Challenge	Caring
Cleanliness	Change
Commitment	Comfort
Competition	Compassion
Cooperation	Connection
Creativity	Courage

Curiosity	Dependability
Determination	Dignity
Discipline	Discretion
Effectiveness	Empathy
Encouragement	Energy
Enjoyment	Enthusiasm
Ethical	Excitement

Dependability	Curiosity
Dignity	Determination
Discretion	Discipline
Empathy	Effectiveness
Energy	Encouragement
Enthusiasm	Enjoyment
Excitement	Ethical

Expertise	Fairness
Faith	Fame
Fashion	Fearlessness
Fidelity	Firmness
Fitness	Flexibility
Flow	Forgiving
Freedom	Friendliness

Fairness	Expertise
Fame	Faith
Fearlessness	Fashion
Firmness	Fidelity
Flexibility	Fitness
Forgiving	Flow
Friendliness	Freedom

Frugality	Fun
Generosity	Genuineness
Giving	Grace
Gratitude	Growth
Harmony	Helpful
Honesty	Honor
Hopeful	Humility

Fun	Frugality
Genuineness	Generosity
Grace	Giving
Growth	Gratitude
Helpful	Harmony
Honor	Honesty
Humility	Hopeful

Humor	Independence
Individuality	Industriousness
Influence	Inspiration
Integrity	Intelligence
Intentional	Intuition
Invention	Joyful
Justice	Kindness

Independence	Humor
Industriousness	Individuality
Inspiration	Influence
Intelligence	Integrity
Intuition	Intentional
Joyful	Invention
Kindness	Justice

Knowledge	Laughter
Leadership	Loving
Loyalty	Making a Difference
Nature	Neatness
Non-Conformity	Nurture
Openness	Optimism
Organization	Passion

Laughter	Knowledge
Loving	Leadership
Making a Difference	Loyalty
Neatness	Nature
Nurture	Non-Conformity
Optimism	Openness
Passion	Organization

Patience	Peace
Perceptive	Perseverance
Planning	Playfulness
Popularity	Power
Pride	Privacy
Quiet	Rationality
Reason	Relaxation

Peace	Patience
Perseverance	Perceptive
Playfulness	Planning
Power	Popularity
Privacy	Pride
Rationality	Quiet
Relaxation	Reason

Reliability	Resilience
Respect	Responsible
Risk	Rules
Safety	Security
Self-Esteem	Self-Control
Self-Knowledge	Sensuality
Simplicity	Sincerity

Resilience	Reliability
Responsible	Respect
Rules	Risk
Security	Safety
Self-Control	Self-Esteem
Sensuality	Self-Knowledge
Sincerity	Simplicity

Skillfullness	Spontaneity
Stability	Strength
Success	Supportive
Teamwork	Thoughtfulness
Tradition	Trust
Truth	Uniqueness
Warmth	Wealth

Spontaneity	Skillfullness
Strength	Stability
Supportive	Success
Thoughtfulness	Teamwork
Trust	Tradition
Uniqueness	Truth
Wealth	Warmth

Wholeheartedness	Wisdom
Worthiness	Add your own:

Wisdom	Wholeheartedness
Add your own:	Worthiness

Value Card Sort Labels

Very Important

Sort of Important

Not Important

Mine

Not Mine

Should

High Priority

Medium Priority

Low Priority

Self-Care

Leisure

Work/Education

Spirituality

Relationships

My Core Values Ranked in Self-Care

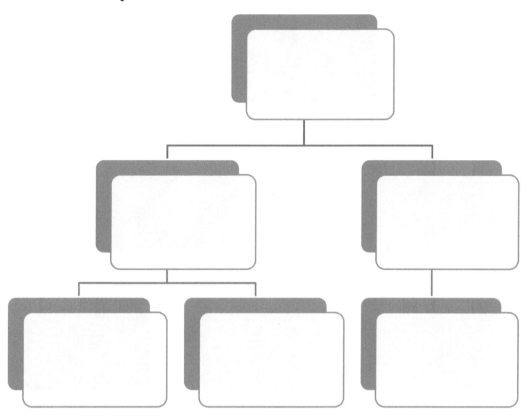

My Core Values Ranked in Leisure

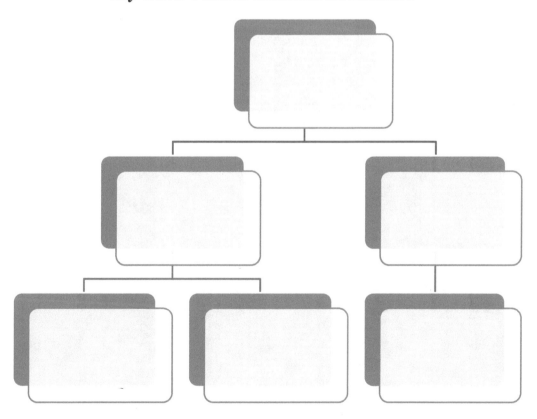

My Core Values Ranked in Work/Education

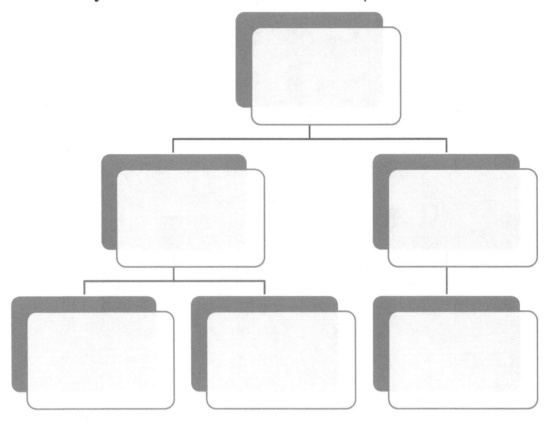

My Core Values Ranked in Spirituality

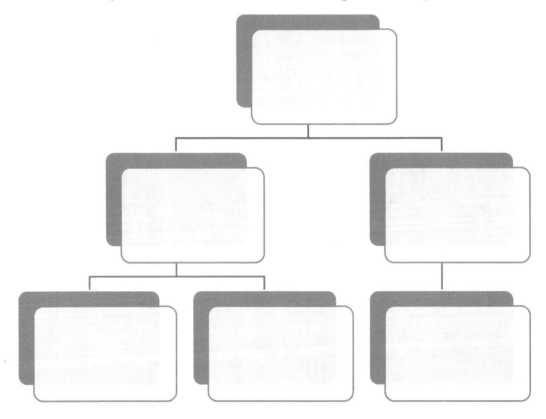

My Core Values Ranked in Relationships

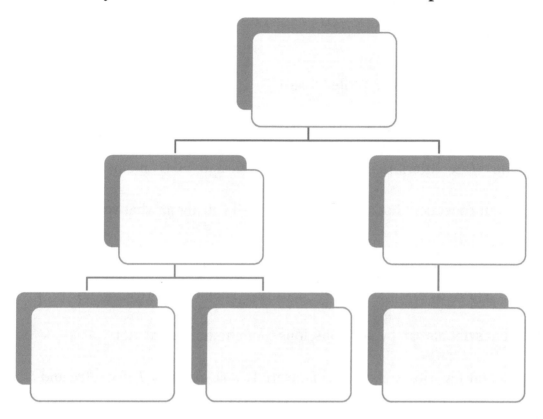

My Core Values Ranked in _____

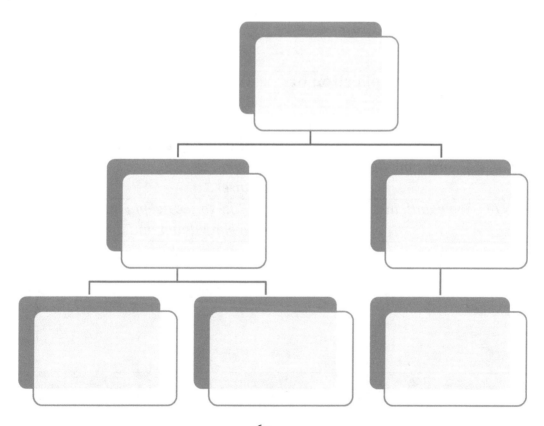

Art as a Doorway

Do you appreciate art? Music? Photography?
Do you make art? Draw? Sing? Write? Read?

Gather art that you appreciate, or even better, that you made. If you haven't made art lately, make some! Or get art you did as a kid. Or look at your Pinterest board. Remember: art is anything you create. Interior design, spreadsheet design, jokes, memes you collect....

Gather up your collection. Look for themes that tell you about what you like and who you are.

Often art we make speaks deeply about us in symbols. Are there colors you choose? What do those colors represent to you? Are there textures? Themes? Stories?

We know that symbols can bypass conscious thought and reveal more to us.

For example, my favorite books as a child were *Where the Wild Things Are* and *Harold and the Purple Crayon*. I now see the therapist and poet in me through these books. In *Where the Wild Things Are* I learned about facing, taming, and befriending fear. Through Harold's Purple Crayon I saw that through creativity we can solve problems and trust ourselves. Now when I write, my poetry reveals things about me that I would not have consciously known on my own.

Themes I see in my art collection or creation	What they Might Mean
Stories about people overcoming hard things creatively	*I have the capacity to be creative in navigating through life.*
Poems that make me slow down and notice	*I tend to rush, and if I slow down, I am wiser.*
Paintings of people with intense eyes	*I like to see deeply into things, and I'd like to slow down and do that more.*

It's your turn:

Themes I see in my art collection or creation	What they Might Mean

Meditations and Guided Visualizations

Here are some guided visualizations that can help you get more ideas or clarity. Feel free to do them often over time.

Start with the container and diaphragmatic breathing exercises on pages 10 and 12.

Once you are settled and relaxed, try one or all of these meditations.

Meditation 1: Talk to Your Future Self
(Developed by Matthew Zell MA, LMHCA, a wonderful therapist)

- Imagine into your future where you are having the life that you want.
- First, notice what you feel like in your mind, body, and emotions in the future life you want.
- Next, expand out. What is around you? Who are you with? What are you doing? Where are you?
- Let the scene fill in. Spend some time in this future that you want.

When you are ready, invite your future self to come back and speak to your present self. What advice or wisdom does your future self have for you?

Take time to write notes.

_____

_____

_____

_____

_____

_____

_____

_____

_____

_____

_____

_____

More thoughts?

Meditation 2: Through Loving Eyes

- Imagine looking into the eyes of someone or some being who loves you deeply. (This could be a person, an animal, a character in a book or movie, or a spiritual figure.)
- See how they look at you with love. See how well they know the real you.
- Spend some time soaking in their loving gaze.
- When you are ready, ask them how they see you.
- What do they want you to know about who you really are?
- What else would they like you to know?
- Ask them if they would give you a gift or a symbol to take with you into your day to represent your experience today.

Take some time to write notes.

_____

_____

_____

_____

_____

_____

_____

_____

_____

_____

_____

_____

_____

_____

_____

_____

_____

_____

_____

_____

_____

More thoughts!

Meditation 3: My Support Team

You know how in the movies, when a team goes in to fight a battle, or take on a boss, or a bully, or an opposing team, there is always a *slow walk* where the hero (or unlikely hero) is flanked by his supporters, and they slowly and confidently walk into battle—or they *slow walk* away after they won the battle?

Who would you have on your team, real or imagined? Create your team of people (living or dead), animals, characters from a book or movie, spiritual figures. Write down who your team is:

_____

_____

_____

Imagine yourself doing the *slow walk* with your team. Where are you going? How do you feel? Take your time to hang out with your team for a while.

Now, notice a few things and write them down.

What quality does each member of your team have, and do you have it too? We don't recognize qualities in others if we don't have them somewhere in ourselves.

Example:

Team Member	Quality	How does that Quality show up in me?
Iron Man	*Innovation, fearlessness*	*I don't feel fearless, but I took risks at work yesterday that others didn't want to take, and I'm pretty creative.*
Oprah	*Not afraid to speak the truth*	*I'm often afraid to speak the truth, but I know it when I see it. Maybe I want to speak up some more.*
My dog	*Loyalty and fun*	*I am a loyal person, and I would like to have more fun.*

Create your support team on the next page.

Meditation 3: My Support Team

Team Member	Quality	How does that Quality show up in me?

Make some notes about what you and your support team were doing and how it felt in your body to imagine it. What might this tell you about yourself?

_____

_____

_____

_____

_____

_____

_____

_____

_____

_____

_____

_____

_____

_____

_____

_____

_____

_____

_____

_____

Meditation 4: Try the Journey to a Wise Person

Make notes about your experience. (See page 30.)

Don't forget to breathe!

Inside/Outside

Draw two pictures:
1. How you see yourself on the inside.
2. How you think others see you from the outside.

How you see yourself on the inside.

Inside/Outside

Draw two pictures:

1. How you see yourself on the inside.
2. How you think others see you from the outside.

How you think others see you from the outside.

Look at your drawings and journal about the following questions.
There are no right answers.

What did you notice?

Look at your drawings and journal about the following questions. There are no right answers.

Does your inside match your outside? If not, is that OK?

_____

_____

_____

_____

_____

_____

_____

_____

_____

_____

_____

_____

_____

_____

_____

_____

_____

_____

_____

_____

_____

_____

_____

_____

_____

_____

Look at your drawings and journal about the following questions. There are no right answers.

Is it true in all situations, or just some?

_____
_____
_____
_____
_____
_____
_____
_____
_____
_____
_____
_____
_____
_____
_____
_____
_____
_____
_____
_____
_____
_____
_____
_____
_____
_____
_____
_____

Look at your drawings and journal about the following questions. There are no right answers.

Do you get lots of feedback about a quality you have that you don't think you have? Might there be any truth to it?

_____
_____
_____
_____
_____
_____
_____
_____
_____
_____
_____
_____
_____
_____
_____
_____
_____
_____
_____
_____
_____
_____
_____
_____
_____
_____
_____
_____

Look at your drawings and journal about the following questions. There are no right answers.

Is there anything about you that you are hiding from the world? If so, is that OK, or would you like to share more?

How did it feel in general to draw yourself? Jot a few thoughts here.

_____

_____

_____

_____

_____

_____

_____

_____

_____

_____

_____

_____

_____

Relationship List

Part of who we are is how we relate to others, and whom we choose to have in our inner circles. Whether you are looking for a partner or wanting to evaluate friendships, thinking ahead can be very helpful.

If you are dating, this is very important because we are actually "high" the first few months of a relationship, with all the chemicals flowing through our brains. This means we have difficulty assessing if a relationship is one that we want.

In the first few months of dating, our brains produce oxytocin. Oxytocin is secreted when we are in love and when we nurse babies. Oxytocin is typically linked to warm, fuzzy feelings, feelings of trust, and is shown in some research to lower stress and anxiety. It helps us bond.

Studies were done in which subjects had oxytocin sprayed into their noses. After the subjects got their dose of oxytocin, strangers came up to them and asked for large amounts of money. The study subjects willingly parted with their money. So, enjoy the high, but be ready to make good decisions about who is right for you, because your brain chemicals may fool you for a while.

Before you meet new people, or if you want to evaluate current relationships, make a *realistic* list of what you want in a partner, what your line in the sand is for things you don't want, and how you want to show up in a relationship. Then evaluate your list and make sure mere humans can meet your wishes and adjust as needed. For example, you might want a goal oriented, kind, organized person who is over 6 feet tall. Maybe you can be with someone shorter? Are any of these desires flexible?

Example:

What I want in a relationship/friendship	What I don't want	How I want to show up
Kindness	*Drug use*	*I want to feel free to be myself.*
Open communication	*Disrespect*	*I want to be appreciated for my gifts.*
Values time together	*Someone who wants me to move to another city*	*I want to feel safe being honest.*
Someone who has an income	*Someone already in a relationship*	*I want to look forward to time together.*
Humor	*Dishonesty*	*I want to have my own friends and activities and be supported in doing so.*

Use your list as your compass to evaluate relationships and people who may be good for you or not good for you.

What I want in a relationship	What I don't want	How I want to show up

Date Yourself

Stop waiting for the perfect date. Create it for yourself.
What would you love to do?

- Do you want to stay in with a bubble bath, good food, and music?
- Do you want to hike up a mountain and watch the sunset?
- Do you want to spend a day in the bookstore reading and watching people?
- Travel?

Write down your perfect date. Make yourself the center of the imaginary date so it does not depend on another person. See what that tells you about yourself, your interests, and wants.

Go ahead and have that date with yourself in real life if you like!

_____

_____

_____

_____

_____

_____

_____

_____

_____

_____

_____

_____

_____

_____

_____

_____

_____

_____

More thoughts?

Uncovering Unhelpful Core Beliefs

Our unconscious belief systems tell us who we are, but they are often wrong. It's hard to get to know the real us when we don't know how to examine our belief systems.

Have you ever met someone who is beautiful but believes they are ugly, or someone really wise who thinks they aren't smart? No matter what you say about their beauty or intelligence, they don't believe you. This is because their unconscious belief system is running the show.

This mind-map exercise is designed to help uncover negative unconscious beliefs that tell us who we are but are not true. Once you know what beliefs you have, you have the power to change them.

First write in the circles (beginning on page 94) all the things that are bugging you. This can be anything from the way your friend chews to a mistake at work.

Underneath each item, write how the situation makes you feel. Angry? Sad? Scared? Hurt? Whatever is true for you. Even if you think you shouldn't be feeling that way, write it down; we all have lots of feelings, and they are all OK.

Underneath the feelings, answer whichever of these questions makes more sense to you (or answer both). Here's the tricky part: **Don't give what should be the logical answer. Answer with the thought that hits you in the gut.** For example, you might know intellectually that you are not alone, that you have family, co-workers, and friends, but the gut answer is "I am alone." Go with that answer.

Here are the questions:

1. What does it mean about you that _____ (fill in the thing that bothers you here). OR
2. What kind of person would experience that thing that bothers you?

For example, if your issue was *My boss was rude to me,* you might write that it made you feel angry and scared.

What does it mean about you that your boss was rude to you?
You might at first think that it's all about him, but your gut answer might be that it means *I'm not important,* or *I'm not respected.*

Then keep asking: *What does it mean that I'm not respected?* or *What kind of person is not respected?* You might then think, *I'm alone* or *I'm worthless.* Keep asking until you feel like you got to the core belief.

Page 102 has some sample core negative beliefs and affirmations you might like. But don't look yet, come up with what's true for you.

Do this for each identified issue and then look for patterns. You'll likely find the same core belief for many scenarios.

See page 100-102 for what to do once you've identified your core beliefs.

See example mind maps on pages 92-93.

Create your own mind maps on pages 94-99.

Issue 1:
My boss was rude to me.

I feel:
Angry
Scared
Righteous
Disrespected

What does it mean about me/what kind of person *has a boss that is rude to them?*
I am not important.
What does it mean/ What kind of person *isn't important?*
I am not seen.
What does it mean/What kind of person *isn't seen?*
I don't matter.
What does it mean about you/What kind of person *doesn't matter?*
Core belief: *I'm alone.*

Issue 2:
My friend was late.

I feel:
Angry
Disrespected
Helpless

What does it mean about me/what kind of person *has friends who are late?*
I am not important.
What does it mean/ What kind of person *isn't important?*
I don't matter.
What does it mean about you/What kind of person *doesn't matter?*
Core belief: *I'm alone.*

Issue 3:
I don't have enough money.

I feel:
Angry
Scared
Embarrassed
Envious

What does it mean about me/what kind of person *doesn't have enough money?*
I'm irresponsible.
What does it mean/ What kind of person *is irresponsible?*
Core belief: *I'm not deserving.*

Issue 4:
I was on hold for an hour with the bank and couldn't get through.

I feel:
Angry
Helpless
Panicked

What does it mean about me/what kind of person *is on hold for an hour with no results?*
I'm a sucker/a loser.
What does it mean/ What kind of person *is a sucker/a loser?*
Core belief: *I don't deserve anything.*

Issue 5:
I'm worried about a health issue.

I feel:
Scared
Alone
Silly (if it's nothing)

What does it mean about me/what kind of person *is worried about a health issue?*
I'm weak.
What does it mean/ What kind of person *is weak?*
Core belief: *I don't deserve good things.*

Issue:

_____

I feel:

_____
_____
_____
_____

What does it mean about me/what kind of person _____?
_____

What does it mean/ What kind of person is _____?
_____

What does it mean/ What kind of person is _____?
_____

Core belief: _____

Issue:

_____

I feel:

_____
_____
_____
_____

What does it mean about me/what kind of person _____?
_____

What does it mean/ What kind of person is _____?
_____

What does it mean/ What kind of person is _____?
_____

Core belief: _____

Issue:

_____

I feel:

_____
_____
_____
_____

What does it mean about me/what kind of person _____?
_____

What does it mean/ What kind of person is _____?
_____

What does it mean/ What kind of person is _____?
_____

Core belief: _____

Issue:

_____

I feel:

_____

_____

_____

_____

What does it mean about me/what kind of person _____?

_____

What does it mean/ What kind of person is _____?

_____

What does it mean/ What kind of person is _____?

_____

Core belief: _____

Issue:

_____

I feel:

_____

_____

_____

_____

What does it mean about me/what kind of person _____?

_____

What does it mean/ What kind of person is _____?

_____

What does it mean/ What kind of person is _____?

_____

Core belief: _____

Issue:

_____

I feel:

_____

_____

_____

_____

What does it mean about me/what kind of person _____?

_____

What does it mean/ What kind of person is _____?

_____

What does it mean/ What kind of person is _____?

_____

Core belief: _____

Issue:
_____

I feel:
_____
_____
_____
_____

What does it mean about me/what kind of person _____?
_____
What does it mean/ What kind of person is _____?
_____
What does it mean/ What kind of person is _____?
_____
Core belief: _____

Issue:
_____

I feel:
_____
_____
_____
_____

What does it mean about me/what kind of person _____?
_____
What does it mean/ What kind of person is _____?
_____
What does it mean/ What kind of person is _____?
_____
Core belief: _____

Issue:
_____

I feel:
_____
_____
_____
_____

What does it mean about me/what kind of person _____?
_____
What does it mean/ What kind of person is _____?
_____
What does it mean/ What kind of person is _____?
_____
Core belief: _____

Issue:

_____

I feel:

_____
_____
_____
_____

What does it mean about me/what kind of person _____ ?

_____

What does it mean/ What kind of person is _____ ?

_____

What does it mean/ What kind of person is _____ ?

_____

Core belief: _____

Issue:

_____

I feel:

_____
_____
_____
_____

What does it mean about me/what kind of person _____ ?

_____

What does it mean/ What kind of person is _____ ?

_____

What does it mean/ What kind of person is _____ ?

_____

Core belief: _____

Issue:

_____

I feel:

_____
_____
_____
_____

What does it mean about me/what kind of person _____ ?

_____

What does it mean/ What kind of person is _____ ?

_____

What does it mean/ What kind of person is _____ ?

_____

Core belief: _____

Issue:
_____

I feel:
_____
_____
_____
_____

What does it mean about me/what kind of person _____?
_____

What does it mean/ What kind of person is _____?
_____

What does it mean/ What kind of person is _____?
_____

Core belief: _____

Issue:
_____

I feel:
_____
_____
_____
_____

What does it mean about me/what kind of person _____?
_____

What does it mean/ What kind of person is _____?
_____

What does it mean/ What kind of person is _____?
_____

Core belief: _____

Issue:
_____

I feel:
_____
_____
_____
_____

What does it mean about me/what kind of person _____?
_____

What does it mean/ What kind of person is _____?
_____

What does it mean/ What kind of person is _____?
_____

Core belief: _____

Issue:

I feel:

What does it mean about me/what kind of person _____?

What does it mean/ What kind of person is _____?

What does it mean/ What kind of person is _____?

Core belief: _____

Issue:

I feel:

What does it mean about me/what kind of person _____?

What does it mean/ What kind of person is _____?

What does it mean/ What kind of person is _____?

Core belief: _____

Issue:

I feel:

What does it mean about me/what kind of person _____?

What does it mean/ What kind of person is _____?

What does it mean/ What kind of person is _____?

Core belief: _____

Challenging Core Beliefs

Oof, these core beliefs can be a gut punch, but now you have control, and they don't get to run the show. Here are some ways to take control so you can be free to explore who you *really* are.

Now that you know your beliefs, you can challenge them. Ask yourself these questions.

- Is this belief helpful?
- Is it true? (If it's a little true then give it a percentage score. Nobody is 100% undeserving or ugly.

Check it out. Ask a trusted friend if they see you this way.

Look for exceptions.

Here are examples of exceptions self-talk:

Negative Belief	Challenge Self Talk/Look for Exceptions
My boss ignored me, so I think I am alone, invisible.	*My boss ignored me once but didn't 7 other times.*
	My worth isn't dependent on him anyway.
	My dog thinks I'm amazing!
	My friend told me she appreciates my humor.

Write your own challenge self-talk:

Negative Belief	Challenge Self Talk/Look for Exceptions

Ignoring Core Beliefs

Our minds will churn out millions of thoughts. **The good news is we don't have to believe them.** Imagine you are standing at the side of a road watching cars go by. These cars are like your thoughts. You see a Volkswagen, two Subarus, a Tesla, a bus. You just watch them go by. You don't get in them and travel to their destination. You don't tell them not to be on the road, you just notice and let them drive on by.

If we treat our negative beliefs this way, we just notice they are there and we don't fight them, but we don't' believe them either. We just realize it's a habit of the mind and go on with our day.

Make your negative core belief a caricature.

If your negative self-talk were a cartoon, what would it look like? What kind of voice would it have? Make it as silly and hyperbolic as possible. It might be a green gremlin with a helium voice. Do you take it seriously now? Give it some humor.

Create Positive Affirmations for Yourself

Post them where you can see them. Repeat them to yourself often. They are fun to say while walking or dancing or to music.

Sample Core beliefs and alternative affirmations:

Negative Belief	More Helpful/True Belief
I am unlovable	I am ok as I am
I am worthless	I am ok as I am
I am inadequate	I can accept myself
I am a failure	I did the best I could
I am responsible for everything	I can recognize appropriate responsibility
I am powerless	I can control what I can even when.....
I'm vulnerable	I can be aware and protect myself most of the time
I can't trust myself	I can learn to trust my judgment
I am discarded/I am alone	I can survive/get my needs met
It's not safe to feel	My feelings are normal and OK/I can choose where and when to express my feelings

Make your own:

Negative Belief	More Helpful/True Belief

Personality Tests

There are many tests online that can help you think about yourself. While no test can pinpoint you as an individual, you can see what they say and think about if they fit.

Here are a few you can Google. There are free online tests or books you can get for each of these.

Myers-Briggs Type Indicator

Through a series of questions, the MBTI assessment helps you identify your natural preferences in four areas of personality:

How do you direct and receive energy—by focusing on the outside world, interacting with people and taking action, or by focusing on your inner world and reflecting on ideas, memories, and experiences?

How do you take in information—by focusing on what you perceive using your five senses or by seeing the big picture and looking for relationships and patterns?

How do you decide and come to conclusions—by logically analyzing the situation or by considering what's important to the people involved?

How do you approach the outside world—in a planned, orderly way or a more flexible, spontaneous way?

Your natural preferences in these four areas sort you into one of 16 distinct MBTI personality types. Understanding these types gives you objective insight that you can use to enhance your professional and personal relationships, as well as your direction, focus, and choices.

Source: https://www.themyersbriggs.com/en-US/Products-and-Services/Myers-Briggs

There are free online Myers-Briggs Tests. Also, the book *Please Understand Me* by David Keirsey has an assessment and walks you through your results.

Enneagram

The Enneagram is a system of personality typing that describes patterns in how people interpret the world and manage their emotions. The Enneagram describes nine personality types and maps each of these types on a nine-pointed diagram, which helps to illustrate how the types relate to one another.

There are free online Enneagram Tests. The book *The Enneagram Made Easy: Discover the 9 Types of People* by Elizabeth Wagele and Renee Baron helps to identify, simplify, and understand your results.

Motivations and Needs Test

Based on Murray's Manifest Needs system, this assessment compares your results with those of thousands of people. This needs profile supports you in knowing yourself better. It is available on Psychology Today online. There is a free version, or you can pay a small amount to get a more detailed report.

So, Now What?

Knowing ourselves is a natural and evolving process. Growing older, having new experiences and relationships continue to shape who we are. I hope you will find these exercises fun and approach them with curiosity throughout your life. Pull them out again and again when you have had life transitions or are feeling like you need centering. I hope they give you a touchstone to enjoy your inner and outer journeys.

Mini-Journal
Here's a writing space for your thoughts on getting Back to *You*.

About the Author

Maureen Kane lives in Bellingham, WA with her family. She is a mental-health therapist in private practice in Washington and Idaho. She is a certified EMDR therapist and an approved EMDR International Association EMDR consultant. She is a Washington State clinical supervisor.

Maureen has been published in many places, including *Time Magazine* and book anthologies. She is a the Boynton Poetry Walk Award winner. Her book of poems is *The Phoenix Requires Ashes: Poems for the Journey*.

Made in United States
Troutdale, OR
01/07/2024